Team Spirit®

THE CHICAGO BLACKHAWKS

BY

MARK STEWART

Content Consultant
Denis Gibbons
Society for International Hockey Research

NORWOOD HOUSE PRESS

CHICAGO, ILLINOIS

Norwood House Press
P.O. Box 316598
Chicago, Illinois 60631

For information regarding Norwood House Press, please visit our website at:
www.norwoodhousepress.com or call 866-565-2900.

PHOTO CREDITS:
All photos courtesy Getty Images except the following:
O-Pee-Chee, Ltd. (6, 23, 40 top, 41 bottom, 43), Société de Publication Merlin (7),
Portnoy/Hockey Hall of Fame (8), Associated Press (19),
Imperial Oil–Turofsky/Hockey Hall of Fame (20),
Hockey Hall of Fame (27), Imperial Oil - Turofsky/Hockey Hall of Fame (31),
Topps, Inc. (9, 21, 22, 35 top left, 36, 38, 40 bottom, 41 top),
Author's Collection (14, 18, 34 right, 35 bottom), Diamond Match, Co. (16, 34 left),
McDiarmid/Cartophilium (17, 30), Bee Hive Golden Corn Syrup (28),
MacFadden Publications, Inc. (29), Chicago Sports Profiles (35 top right),
Hockey Pictorial (41 left), Matt Richman (48).
Cover photo: Bill Smith/Getty Images
Special thanks to Topps, Inc.

Editor: Mike Kennedy
Designer: Ron Jaffe
Project Management: Black Book Partners, LLC.
Research: Joshua Zaffos
Special thanks to Bobby Hall

LIBRARY OF CONGRESS CATALOGING-IN-PUBLICATION DATA

Stewart, Mark, 1960-
    The Chicago Blackhawks / by Mark Stewart.
        p. cm.
    Includes bibliographical references and index.
    Summary: "Presents the history and accomplishments of the Chicago
Blackhawks hockey team. Includes highlights of players, coaches, and
awards, quotes, timeline, maps, glossary and websites"--Provided by
publisher.
    ISBN-13: 978-1-59953-337-7 (library edition : alk. paper)
    ISBN-10: 1-59953-337-5 (library edition : alk. paper) 1. Chicago
Blackhawks (Hockey team)--History--Juvenile literature. I. Title.
    GV848.C48S78 2009
    796.962'640977311--dc22
                                                              2009014715

COVER PHOTO: The Blackhawks celebrate a victory with their fans during the
2008–09 season.

Table of Contents

SPORTS WORDS & VOCABULARY WORDS: In this book, you will find many words that are new to you. You may also see familiar words used in new ways. The glossary on page 46 gives the meanings of hockey words, as well as "everyday" words that have special hockey meanings. These words appear in **bold type** throughout the book. The glossary on page 47 gives the meanings of vocabulary words that are not related to hockey. They appear in ***bold italic type*** throughout the book.

Meet the Blackhawks

The difference between winning and losing in hockey often comes down to toughness. Victory also depends on a team doing all the "little things" right. The Chicago Blackhawks play as hard and as smart as any team in the **National Hockey League (NHL)**. Through aches and pains, and bumps and bruises, they skate at full speed whenever they take the ice.

Chicago fans expect maximum effort from the Blackhawks. They cheer as loudly for a great body check or defensive play as they do for an incredible goal. It is part of a *tradition* that stretches back more than 80 years.

This book tells the story of the Blackhawks. They have had some amazing players and won some heart-stopping games. The most famous Blackhawks are known for being excellent **all-around** stars. The team is at its best when each player hopping over the boards is ready to do whatever it takes to win.

Martin Havlat, Brian Campbell, and Matt Walker celebrate a goal during the 2008–09 season.

Way Back When

When the NHL began in 1917, all of its teams were located in Canada. Each year, the league champion played the winners of other leagues for the sport's greatest prize, the **Stanley Cup**. Some of the best teams outside of the NHL played in the United States, where hockey was also a popular sport.

By the mid-1920s, the NHL was the last surviving **professional** hockey league. The NHL, however, also faced troubled times. To increase its popularity, the league added several U.S. teams. One of these clubs was the Chicago Blackhawks. They joined the league for the 1926–27 season, along with the New York Rangers and Detroit Cougars. That gave the NHL 10 teams in all.

ALL-TIME GREATS

CHUCK GARDINER

The Blackhawks had some of the league's top players, including high-scoring Johnny Gottselig and a pesky right wing named Mush March, who stood just 5′ 5″. Goalie Chuck Gardiner was one of the best in the business. This trio led the Blackhawks to the Stanley Cup in 1933–34. Chicago won the championship again four years later. *Burly* Earl Seibert scored goals and

LEFT: A trading card of Chuck Gardiner.
RIGHT: Stan Mikita, one of the top players in team history.

played great defense, while Mike Karakas starred in goal.

The Blackhawks of the 1930s were unusual because of the number of Americans they had in uniform. Most teams had only one or two players born in the United States, if any at all. Chicago owner Frederic McLaughlin wanted to promote American hockey. He signed every U.S. player he could find.

During the 1940s, the Blackhawks were led by several players destined for the **Hall of Fame**, including Bill Mosienko, Clint Smith, and the Bentley brothers, Max and Doug. During the 1950s, however, the Blackhawks did not have a single winning season. Things began to change when center Stan Mikita, goalie Glenn Hall, and defenseman Pierre Pilote joined the club. In 1960–61, Chicago won its third Stanley Cup.

The team's star of stars was 22-year-old Bobby Hull. The "Golden Jet" *electrified* fans. Hull was a lightning-fast skater who never slowed down. He had arms like sledgehammers and a body like an *anvil*.

No one could bump him off the puck. Hull's slapshot exploded off his stick at over 110 miles per hour (161 kilometers per hour). If a goalie blinked, the puck was past him!

The Blackhawks returned to the **Stanley Cup Finals** in 1962, and again in 1971 and 1973. By the 1970s, one of their top players was an acrobatic goalie named Tony Esposito. Along with defensemen Keith Magnuson, Bill White, Pat Stapleton, and Doug Wilson, "Tony O" made the Blackhawks hard to score against.

Still, nearly two *decades* passed before Chicago was a serious title *contender* again. In the spring of 1992, four stars— defenseman Chris Chelios, goalie Ed Belfour, right wing Steve Larmer, and center Jeremy Roenick—guided the team back to the Stanley Cup Finals. Within a few seasons, however, the Blackhawks were struggling again. In 1997–98, Chicago missed the **playoffs** for the first time in 29 years. A once proud team was on the verge of collapse. It would take a new owner, a new attitude, and a load of team spirit to lift the Blackhawks back to the top of the NHL.

LEFT: Bobby Hull speeds up the ice.
ABOVE: Jeremy Roenick, one of the stars who led the Blackhawks to the 1992 Stanley Cup Finals.

The Team Today

There is an old saying that goes, "Like father, like son." It means that a young boy often grows up to be just like his dad. Chicago hockey fans hoped that would *not* be the case when Rocky Wirtz took over the team in 2007. His father, Bill, had been the owner of the Blackhawks, but he wasn't popular with the fans.

Rocky made many changes and brought back great players such as Bobby Hull and Stan Mikita to work for the team. The Blackhawks began rebuilding with young stars, including Jonathan Toews and Patrick Kane, and **veterans** such as Brian Campbell and Martin Havlat.

The team also began reaching out to fans with fun events. In no time, the Blackhawks were winning again, and the team's arena was full every night. After years of empty seats, the Blackhawks had the highest attendance in the NHL in 2008–09! Chicago was ready to make a run for another Stanley Cup.

Patrick Kane, Duncan Keith, and team captain Jonathan Toews congratulate Troy Brouwer after a goal during the 2008–09 season.

Home Ice

From 1929 to 1994, the Blackhawks played their home games in the Chicago Stadium. When it opened, the Chicago Stadium was the largest indoor arena in the world. It was also the first to have air-conditioning, which sometimes created fog over the rink! When the Chicago Stadium got too old, it was torn down. Many people watched the demolition with tears in their eyes.

Today, the Blackhawks play in a new stadium. It was completed in 1994 and named the United Center. The team wanted the new stadium to be a great place to watch a game, just like the old stadium. Fans especially liked how loud it was inside. The Blackhawks' arena was actually designed to *amplify* noise.

BY THE NUMBERS

- *The Blackhawks' arena has 20,500 seats for hockey.*
- *It cost $175 million to build in 1994.*
- *As of 2009, six uniform numbers have been retired by the team: #1 (Glenn Hall), #3 (Pierre Pilote and Keith Magnuson), #9 (Bobby Hull), #18 (Denis Savard), #21 (Stan Mikita), and #35 (Tony Esposito). A seventh number, #99 (for Wayne Gretzky), was retired by the entire NHL.*

The Blackhawks chase down the puck against the Colorado Avalanche during a 2006–07 game in Chicago's arena.

Dressed for Success

The Blackhawks have always used a *logo* and colors that honor the Native American culture of their home state of Illinois. The team's name comes from Chief Black Hawk of the Sauk nation. Chicago's first owner, Frederic McLaughlin, served in an army unit in World War I that was nicknamed the Blackhawks. When he started his hockey club a few years later, he already had a name picked out.

The team's logo shows the head of Chief Black Hawk. For the first 30 years, the design was set inside a circle. In 1955, the team changed its uniform to look the way it does today. It is one of the most popular uniforms in sports. The Blackhawks' jersey is worn by fans all over the world, even by people who don't follow hockey.

Harry Watson models the team's road uniform from the early 1950s.

UNIFORM BASICS

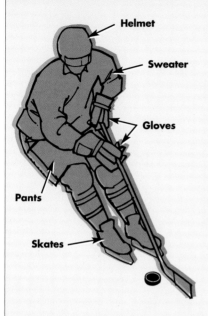

The hockey uniform has five important parts:

- Helmet
- Sweater
- Pants
- Gloves
- Skates

Hockey helmets are made of hard plastic with softer padding inside. Some players also wear visors to protect their eyes.

The hockey uniform top is called a sweater. Players wear padding underneath it to protect their shoulders, spine, and ribs. Padded hockey pants, or "breezers," extend from the waist to the knees. Players also wear padding on their knees and shins.

Hockey gloves protect the top of the hand and the wrist. Only a thin layer of leather covers the palm, which helps a player control his stick. A goalie wears two different gloves—one for catching pucks and one for blocking them. Goalies also wear heavy leg pads and a mask. They paint their masks to match their personalities and team colors.

All players wear hockey skates. The blade is curved at each end. The skate "boot" is made from metal, plastic, nylon, and either real or *synthetic* leather. Goalies wear skates that have extra protection on the toe and ankle.

Kris Versteeg wears the team's road uniform during a 2008–09 game.

We Won!

Of Chicago's three Stanley Cups, two came during the 1930s. Back then, the slapshot had not yet been invented, so the best way to score was through a combination of hard skating, crisp passing, and a little trickery from time to time. The Blackhawks had all three going for them—along with a rock-solid defense.

In 1934, the Blackhawks reached the Stanley Cup Finals by first defeating the Montreal Canadiens in the playoffs. The Canadiens

HAROLD MARCH

"Black Hawks"

were no match for Chicago's top line of Mush March, Doc Romnes, and Paul Thompson. March netted the winning goal in the two-game series. The Blackhawks next beat Montreal's other team, the Maroons. This time, goalie Chuck Gardiner and defensemen Sid Abel and Lionel Conacher led the charge.

For just the second time in history, the Stanley Cup Finals featured two American teams, the Blackhawks and Detroit Red Wings. Chicago's defense was the difference in the series, which the Blackhawks won in four games. Two of their victories came in **overtime**. March fired the

shot that sealed the championship—a bullet through the legs of the Detroit goalie.

Four years later, the Blackhawks made another amazing run to the Stanley Cup. Chicago's coach for the 1937–38 season was a baseball umpire named Bill Stewart. His main hockey experience was as a referee. The fans howled their disapproval when Stewart moved star defender Earl Seibert up to the wing. Then the team stumbled to a 14–25–9 record and barely made the playoffs.

Things changed once the **postseason** started. In the first round, goalie Mike Karakas played brilliantly against the Canadiens. The Blackhawks won the series in three games. The key goal came off the stick of Seibert. Suddenly, fans began calling the Blackhawks the "Wonder Team." They lived up to this name against the New York Americans in the next round. Chicago dropped the first game but won the next two to reach the Stanley Cup Finals. The star of the series was Alex Levinsky, the defenseman who replaced Seibert!

Against the Toronto Maple Leafs in the finals, the Blackhawks continued their amazing run. Even injuries to Karakas and Romnes

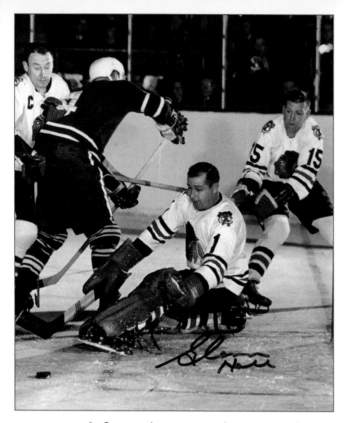

could not stop them. Karakas hurt his foot and took the ice in a special skate. Romnes broke his nose and wore a football helmet to protect his face. Chicago won the series in four games. Stewart was carried off the ice on the shoulders of his *jubilant* players.

There was nothing surprising about the Blackhawks in 1960–61. Goalie Glenn Hall **anchored** a defense that starred Pierre Pilote and Elmer Vasko. Stan Mikita, Bobby Hull, Red Hay, Murray Balfour, Ken Wharram, and team captain Ed Litzenberger were the club's top scorers.

The Blackhawks faced the Red Wings in the Stanley Cup Finals that year. Hockey fans prepared for a showdown between the two best players in the game, Hull and Detroit's Gordie Howe. Hull scored twice in Game 1 to give his team a 3–2 victory. Howe set up a pair of goals in Game 2, and Detroit won 3–1.

The teams traded victories again, and the series remained tied. In Game 5, the Blackhawks cruised to a 6–3 blowout in front of a stomping, screaming Chicago crowd.

It looked as if the Red Wings would win Game 6 in Detroit. They led 1–0 in the second period and then went on the power play. Chicago's Reg Fleming knew the Red Wings would try to get a shot for Howe. He stole a pass meant for the Detroit star, headed down the ice on a breakaway, and scored a spectacular goal. The Blackhawks went on to win 5–1 and celebrated their third Stanley Cup.

LEFT: A photo autographed by Glenn Hall shows him making a save.
ABOVE: Bobby Hull and Jack Evans pose with the Stanley Cup after Chicago's 1961 championship.

Go-To Guys

To be a true star in the NHL, you need more than a great slapshot. You have to be a "go-to guy"—someone teammates trust to make the winning play when the seconds are ticking away in a big game. Blackhawks fans have had a lot to cheer about over the years, including these great stars ...

THE PIONEERS

CHUCK GARDINER   Goalie

- BORN: DECEMBER 31, 1904 • DIED: JUNE 13, 1934
- PLAYED FOR TEAM: 1927–28 TO 1933–34

When Chuck Gardiner began his NHL career, he studied the best shooters until he knew all their moves. He also used his quick hands and feet to his advantage. Gardiner had 42 **shutouts** in seven seasons before he died tragically at the age of 29.

EARL SEIBERT   Defenseman

- BORN: DECEMBER 7, 1911 • DIED: MAY 12, 1990
- PLAYED FOR TEAM: 1935–36 TO 1944–45

Earl Seibert was a great all-around player who helped Chicago to its second Stanley Cup. He was a fearless shot blocker, a powerful skater, and a good passer. Seibert was an **All-Star** nine years in a row with the Blackhawks.

ABOVE: Earl Seibert   **RIGHT**: Stan Mikita

PIERRE PILOTE   Defenseman

• BORN: DECEMBER 11, 1931   • PLAYED FOR TEAM: 1955–56 TO 1967–68

Pierre "Pete" Pilote loved to deliver crushing **hipchecks**. He loved sending fast-skating forwards spinning down the ice. Pilote also handled the puck extremely well. He teamed with Elmer Vasko to form the league's best defensive duo in the early 1960s.

GLENN HALL   Goalie

• BORN: OCTOBER 3, 1931   • PLAYED FOR TEAM: 1957–58 TO 1966–67

Glenn Hall helped introduce a new style of goaltending. He would often leave the net to cut down a shooter's angle or retrieve a loose puck. In addition, Hall was almost *indestructible*. He played 502 games in a row for the Blackhawks.

BOBBY HULL   Left Wing

• BORN: JANUARY 3, 1939   • PLAYED FOR TEAM: 1957–58 TO 1971–72

Few players were faster or stronger than Bobby Hull. He also had the hardest slapshot in the game—maybe the hardest ever. He led the NHL in goals seven times.

STAN MIKITA   Center

• BORN: MAY 20, 1940

• PLAYED FOR TEAM: 1958–59 TO 1979–80

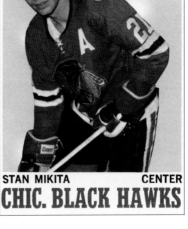

STAN MIKITA   CENTER
CHIC. BLACK HAWKS

If an opponent had a weakness, Stan Mikita would find it. He did not have blinding speed, but he was a skilled passer and shooter. His ability to out-think opponents was legendary. Mikita was one of the first players to master the art of shooting with a curved stick.

TONY ESPOSITO   Goalie

- BORN: APRIL 23, 1943 • PLAYED FOR TEAM: 1969–70 TO 1983–84

As a **rookie**, Tony Esposito set a record with 15 shutouts and led the Blackhawks to the playoffs. For the next 13 years, it was the same story—"Tony O" was between the pipes, and Chicago made the postseason. His flop-to-the-ice style was copied by a ***generation*** of netminders.

DENIS SAVARD   Center

- BORN: FEBRUARY 4, 1961
- PLAYED FOR TEAM: 1980–81 TO 1989–90 & 1994–95 TO 1996–97

DENIS SAVARD•C

Denis Savard recorded three **assists** in his first NHL game. He scored 30 or more goals for Chicago seven years in a row. His favorite move was the Spin-O-Rama—Savard would catch the defense off-guard by spinning completely around and then surprising the goalie with a shot.

JEREMY ROENICK   Center

- BORN: JANUARY 17, 1970
- PLAYED FOR TEAM: 1988–89 TO 1995–96

Chicago fans loved Jeremy Roenick for his goal scoring. They adored him for his funny and outrageous personality. Roenick scored 40-plus goals in a season four times for the Blackhawks and more than 50 twice.

CHRIS CHELIOS   Defenseman

- BORN: JANUARY 25, 1962
- PLAYED FOR TEAM: 1990–91 TO 1998–99

The Blackhawks traded Denis Savard to get Chris Chelios in 1990. The deal paid off right away, when Chicago rose to the top of the **standings** for the first time since the 1960s. Opponents rarely challenged Chelios. In one-on-one battles, he won almost every time.

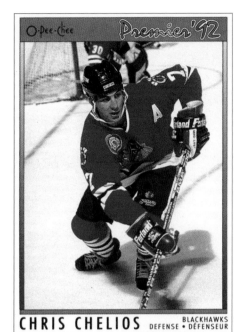

CHRIS CHELIOS DEFENSE • DÉFENSEUR BLACKHAWKS

JONATHAN TOEWS   Center

- BORN: APRIL 29, 1988
- FIRST SEASON WITH TEAM: 2007–08

The Blackhawks chose Jonathan Toews with the third pick in the 2006 NHL **draft**. In 2008, he became the third-youngest player in league history to be named a team captain. Toews was voted to the starting lineup of the 2009 **All-Star Game**.

PATRICK KANE   Right Wing

- BORN: NOVEMBER 19, 1988 • FIRST SEASON WITH TEAM: 2007–08

In 2007, the Blackhawks had the top pick in the NHL draft for the first time ever. They chose Patrick Kane. In his second game, he beat superstar Dominik Hasek and the Detroit Red Wings with a game-winning shootout goal. Kane finished with 72 points (21 goals plus 51 assists) that season and won the Calder Trophy as the league's top rookie.

LEFT: Denis Savard   **ABOVE**: Chris Chelios

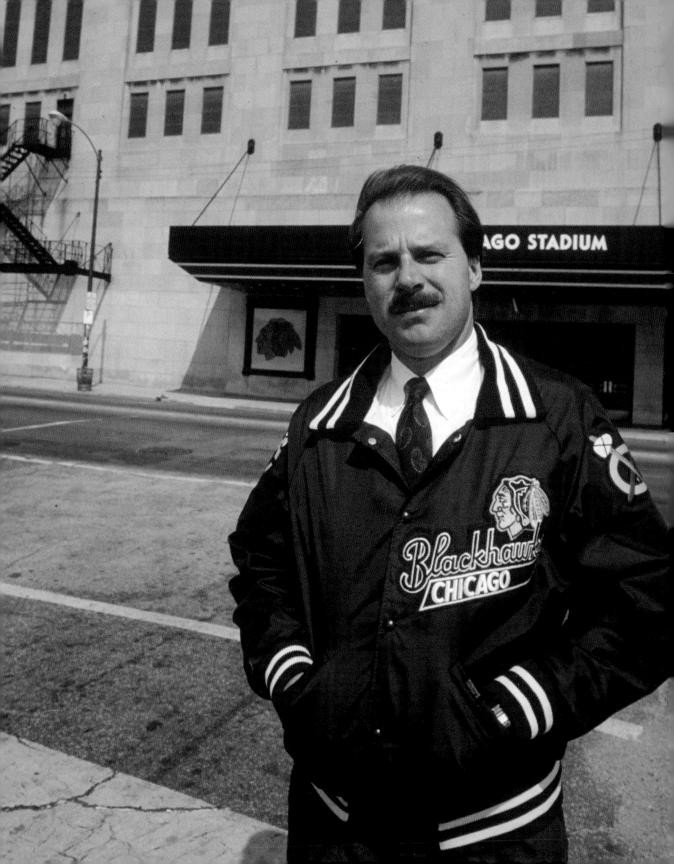

Behind the Bench

When a team has been around as long as the Blackhawks, it is no surprise that some of the sport's best coaches have stood behind their bench. Among the most successful were Tommy Gorman, Bill Stewart, and Rudy Pilous. Each guided the Blackhawks to the Stanley Cup.

The man who logged the most seasons in Chicago was Billy Reay. He took over the team in 1963–64 and stayed until the late 1970s—14 years in all. Reay had just one losing season during that time. He led the Blackhawks to the Stanley Cup Finals three times.

Mike Keenan was just as famous—and successful—in his work as the coach of the Blackhawks. Keenan was super-tough. When he came to Chicago in 1988–89, the Blackhawks were a losing team. Keenan whipped them into a Stanley Cup contender. He coached the Blackhawks to the **Western Conference Finals** in his first two seasons. In his fourth and last season, "Iron Mike" led Chicago all the way to the Stanley Cup Finals.

Mike Keenan, the coach who led the Blackhawks to the Stanley Cup Finals in 1992.

One Great Day

Things were not looking good for the Blackhawks as they prepared for the 1938 Stanley Cup Finals against the Toronto Maple Leafs. Chicago reached the championship round with surprising victories in its first two playoff series. But those wins came at a high cost. Goalie Mike Karakas broke a toe. With Game 1 in Toronto approaching, he was in great pain. His foot was so swollen that he could not even put on his skate.

NHL teams did not carry extra goalies in the 1930s. The rules stated that a team with an injured goalie could find a replacement, as long as the opponent agreed. Davey Kerr of the New York Rangers happened to be in the crowd at Maple Leaf Gardens that night. Kerr offered to play for Chicago, but Conn Smythe—the man who ran the Maple Leafs—refused. Instead, he told the Blackhawks that they had to use a Toronto **minor leaguer** named Alfie Moore.

Moore's nickname was "Half-Pint" because he stood barely over five feet tall. As Moore suited up, he apologized to his new teammates and admitted that they got a bad deal. When he saw Smythe before

26

Mike Karakas poses for a photo. A foot injury forced him out of Game 1 of the 1938 Stanley Cup Finals, but Alfie Moore saved the day for Chicago.

the game began, he shouted, "I hope I stop every puck you fellows fire at me—even if I have to eat the rubber!"

Smythe had **unleashed** a wildcat. After allowing an early goal to Toronto, Moore was like a brick wall. Meanwhile, Johnny Gottselig scored twice and Paul Thompson once to give Chicago a 3–1 victory.

After the game, the Maple Leafs were stunned. The Blackhawks were full of confidence. When Karakas returned to the ice, they went on to win the Stanley Cup.

Legend Has It

Stan Mikita

Was Stanislav Gvoth the Blackhawks' top career scorer?

LEGEND HAS IT that he was. Of course, Chicago fans know him as Stan Mikita. In 1948, when the Soviet army seized control of Czechoslovakia, Mikita's parents sent him to live with his aunt and uncle in Canada. The eight-year-old took the name of his relatives, Mikita. He ended his career with 1,467 points—more than anyone else in team history.

ABOVE: Stan Mikita, whose real name was Stanislav Gvoth.
RIGHT: Doug and Max Bentley were front-page news during the 1940s.

Did three brothers ever play together on the same line?

LEGEND HAS IT that they did. On New Year's Day in 1943, Max, Doug, and Reg Bentley skated together against the New York Rangers. It was the first time an "all-brothers" line took the ice in an NHL game. Chicago won 6–5, but the "Bentley" experiment soon ended, and the line was broken up.

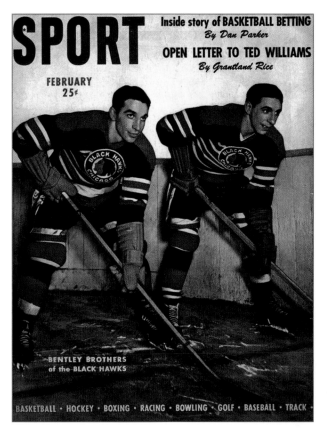

SPORT

Inside story of BASKETBALL BETTING
By Dan Parker

OPEN LETTER TO TED WILLIAMS
By Grantland Rice

FEBRUARY
25¢

BENTLEY BROTHERS
of the BLACK HAWKS

BASKETBALL · HOCKEY · BOXING · RACING · BOWLING · GOLF · BASEBALL · TRACK

Who was the NHL's greatest "clutch" rookie?

LEGEND HAS IT that Steve Larmer was. A **clutch** player scores goals when his team needs them the most. In 1982–83, Larmer netted nine game-winning goals—more than any rookie in NHL history. Larmer was very quick and had a powerful shot. He was one of the few right wings who shot left-handed.

It Really Happened

Chicago fans had little to cheer about during the 1951–52 season. The team won only 17 games and finished in last place—for the fifth time in six seasons. But those who watched the final game of the year were treated to the most amazing 21 seconds of hockey they had ever seen.

The Blackhawks were playing the New York Rangers in Madison Square Garden. They trailed 6–2 in the third period when Chicago's

Gus Bodnar won a faceoff in the Rangers' end. Bodnar slid the puck to Bill Mosienko. The fun was about to begin.

Mosienko was one of the few bright spots for the Blackhawks in the 1950s. At the beginning of the game, he stood fourth in the NHL in goals with 28. Mosienko took Bodnar's pass and cracked a shot past goalie Lorne Anderson to make the score 6–3.

The players skated to center ice for the next faceoff. Bodnar won it again and got the

ABOVE: Bill Mosienko **RIGHT**: Mosienko shows off his skating skills.

puck back to Mosienko, who streaked toward the Rangers' goal. Once again he fired a shot past Anderson. Now the score was 6–4. Only 11 seconds had passed.

Mosienko wasn't done. Ten seconds later, he scored again for a **hat trick**. His goals came at 6:09, 6:20, and 6:30—or over a span of only 21 seconds. No one before or since has come close to matching this feat. Chicago went on to win 7–6. When the game was over, Mosienko had passed Ted Lindsay and Bernie Geoffrion on the scoring list. He finished the year second in the league with 31 goals.

Team Spirit

Chicago hockey fans are some of the loudest and proudest on the planet. When the Blackhawks score, the Chicago crowd shakes the building with its cheers. When the team played in the Chicago Stadium (on Madison Street), the arena was called the "Madhouse on Madison." Thanks to noisy fans and a gigantic pipe organ, there was never a quiet moment there!

In their new home, Chicago fans are just as noisy. They were thrilled when the team installed an organ, even though it took a couple of seasons to make it as loud as the one at the Chicago Stadium.

When the music starts, so does Tommy Hawk, the team's *mascot*. Tommy is a giant hawk who roams through the stands wearing a Chicago jersey. If Tommy thinks fans are too laid-back, look out— he will give them a Silly String shower! Between seasons, fans can connect one-on-one with Tommy and the Blackhawks. In recent years, the team has held big events where the players mix with the public. It is one of the hottest tickets in town.

Tommy Hawk gets the fans excited during a 2008–09 game played outdoors at Chicago's Wrigley Field.

33

Timeline

The hockey season is played from October through June. That means each season takes place at the end of one year and the beginning of the next. In this timeline, the accomplishments of the Blackhawks are shown by season.

1933–34
The Blackhawks win the Stanley Cup.

1942–43
Doug Bentley is the team's first scoring champion.

1926–27
The Blackhawks play their first NHL season.

1937–38
The team wins its second Stanley Cup.

1953–54
Goalie Al Rollins wins the Hart Trophy as the NHL's top player.

JOHNNY GOTTSELIG
"Black Hawks"

Johnny Gottselig, a star for the team in the 1930s.

Frederic McLaughlin, the team owner in the 1930s.

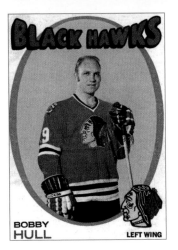
Bobby
Hull

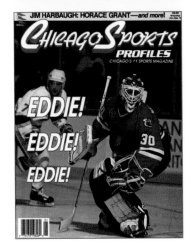
Eddie
Belfour

1965–66
Bobby Hull becomes the first player to score more than 50 goals in a season.

1990–91
Ed Belfour wins the **Vezina Trophy** and Calder Trophy.

2008–09
Jonathan Toews becomes team captain at age 20.

1960–61
Chicago wins its third Stanley Cup.

1972–73
The Blackhawks reach the Stanley Cup Finals for the second time in three seasons.

A souvenir photo of the 1961 NHL champions.

Fun Facts

JUST ONE WORD

For most of the team's history, its name was usually spelled as two words: Black Hawks. In 1986, Chicago discovered that its original papers from 1926 had its name written out as one word. Since then the team name has been spelled *Blackhawks*.

HANDS UP

Before Billy Reay coached the Blackhawks, he was already famous for something players now do every day. Reay was the first player to thrust his arms in the air after a goal.

SONG BIRD

After the Blackhawks drafted Patrick Kane in 2007, he became an "honorary" Chicagoan by singing "Take Me Out to the Ball Game" at a Cubs baseball game. He also threw out the first pitch that day.

ABOVE: Billy Reay

MUSIC MAN

One of the most beloved Blackhawks never skated for the team. Al Melgard, the organist at the Chicago Stadium, entertained fans for four decades starting in the 1930s. He got the job after impressing the team with his quick thinking. Melgard stopped a riot at a boxing match by playing the Star Spangled Banner!

ON THE TUBE

During the 1946–47 season, the Blackhawks became the first team to televise its games. Fans could watch them on WBKB, a Chicago TV station at the time.

IT'S ABOUT TIME

In February of 1935, Lorne Chabot became the first hockey player to make the cover of *TIME* magazine. Chabot had replaced Chicago goalie Chuck Gardiner, who died from an injury not related to hockey after leading the team to the Stanley Cup the year before.

PERFECT GENTLEMEN

In 1944–45, Bill Mosienko and Clint Smith had 54 points each. Neither player spent a minute in the penalty box that season.

Talking Hockey

"Somewhere in my wild childhood I must have done something right."

> —*Bobby Hull, on living his boyhood dream of playing in the NHL*

"We were proof that '**chemistry**' was more than a *cliché*. It is crucial to the success of a line."

> —*Dennis Hull, on playing with Pit Martin and Jim Pappin on Chicago's "MPH Line" in the 1960s and 1970s*

"That whole season was something special—both for the Blackhawks and for me personally."

> —*Tony Esposito, on his amazing rookie year in 1969–70*

"Our first priority was staying alive. Our second was stopping the puck."

> —*Glenn Hall, on what it was like in the days before goalies wore masks*

ABOVE: Dennis Hull   **RIGHT**: Patrick Kane and Jonathan Toews

38

"I'm the kind of guy who wants the puck, who can make my teammates better."

—Jonathan Toews, on his ability as a leader

"I realized how hard you have to work in order to win."

*—Dirk Graham, on learning from the team's loss in the
1992 Stanley Cup Finals*

"There are rough players and there are dirty players. I'm rough and dirty."

—Stan Mikita, on his early days as a "tough guy" in the NHL

"I'm looking forward to our Cup runs in the future!"

—Patrick Kane, on the future of the Blackhawks

For the Record

T he great Blackhawks teams and players have left their marks on the record books. These are the "best of the best" …

Bobby Hull

Glenn Hall

BLACKHAWKS AWARD WINNERS

HART MEMORIAL TROPHY
MOST VALUABLE PLAYER (MVP)

Max Bentley	1945–46
Al Rollins	1953–54
Bobby Hull	1964–65
Bobby Hull	1965–66
Stan Mikita	1966–67
Stan Mikita	1967–68

CALDER TROPHY
TOP ROOKIE PLAYER

Cully Dahlstrom	1937–38
Ed Litzenberger	1954–55
Red Hay	1959–60
Tony Esposito	1969–70
Steve Larmer	1982–83
Ed Belfour	1990–91
Patrick Kane	2007–08

ART ROSS TROPHY
TOP SCORER

Roy Conacher	1948–49
Bobby Hull	1959–60
Bobby Hull	1961–62
Stan Mikita	1963–64
Stan Mikita	1964–65
Bobby Hull	1965–66
Stan Mikita	1966–67
Stan Mikita	1967–68

VEZINA TROPHY
TOP GOALTENDER

Chuck Gardiner	1931–32
Chuck Gardiner	1933–34
Lorne Chabot	1934–35
Glenn Hall	1962–63
Glenn Hall*	1966–67
Denis DeJordy	1966–67
Tony Esposito	1969–70
Tony Esposito & Gary Smith	1971–72
Tony Esposito*	1973–74
Ed Belfour	1990–91
Ed Belfour	1992–93

JAMES NORRIS MEMORIAL TROPHY
TOP DEFENSIVE PLAYER

Pierre Pilote	1962–63
Pierre Pilote	1963–64
Pierre Pilote	1964–65
Doug Wilson	1981–82
Chris Chelios	1992–93
Chris Chelios	1995–96

ALL-STAR GAME MVP

Bobby Hull	1969–70
Bobby Hull	1970–71
Eric Daze	2001–02

* Tied another player for the award.

BLACKHAWKS ACHIEVEMENTS

ACHIEVEMENT	SEASON
Stanley Cup Finalists	1930–31
Stanley Cup Champions	1933–34
Stanley Cup Champions	1937–38
Stanley Cup Finalists	1943–44
Stanley Cup Champions	1960–61
Stanley Cup Finalists	1961–62
Stanley Cup Finalists	1964–65
Stanley Cup Finalists	1970–71
Stanley Cup Finalists	1972–73
Stanley Cup Finalists	1991–92

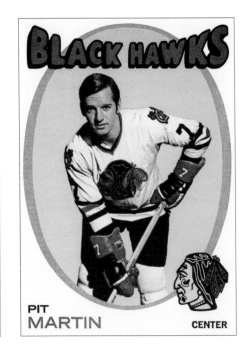

BLACK HAWKS

PIT MARTIN   CENTER

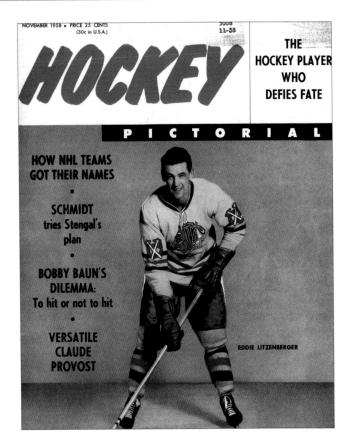

NOVEMBER 1958 • PRICE 25 CENTS
(30c in U.S.A.)

5008
11-58

HOCKEY

THE HOCKEY PLAYER WHO DEFIES FATE

PICTORIAL

HOW NHL TEAMS GOT THEIR NAMES
•
SCHMIDT tries Stengal's plan
•
BOBBY BAUN'S DILEMMA: To hit or not to hit
•
VERSATILE CLAUDE PROVOST

EDDIE LITZENBERGER

Pierre Pilote

CHICAGO BLACK HAWKS DEFENSE

TOP: Pit Martin, a key member of the 1970–71 and 1972–73 teams.
ABOVE: Pierre Pilote
LEFT: Ed Litzenberger, who starred with Pilote for the 1961 champs.

41

Pinpoints

The history of a hockey team is made up of many smaller stories. These stories take place all over the map—not just in the city a team calls "home." Match the pushpins on these maps to the Team Facts and you will begin to see the story of the Blackhawks unfold!

TEAM FACTS

1 Chicago, Illinois—*The Blackhawks have played here since 1926.*

2 Aurora, Minnesota—*Mike Karakas was born here.*

3 Buffalo, New York—*Patrick Kane was born here.*

4 Boston, Massachusetts—*Jeremy Roenick was born here.*

5 Kenogami, Quebec, Canada—*Pierre Pilote was born here.*

6 Sault Ste. Marie, Ontario, Canada—*Tony Esposito was born here.*

7 Pointe Ann, Ontario, Canada—*Bobby and Dennis Hull were born here.*

8 Carman, Manitoba, Canada—*Ed Belfour was born here.*

9 Winnipeg, Manitoba, Canada—*Bill Mosienko was born here.*

10 Humboldt, Saskatchewan, Canada—*Glenn Hall was born here.*

11 Edinburgh, Scotland—*Chuck Gardiner was born here.*

12 Sokolce, Czechoslovakia*—*Stan Mikita was born here.*

*Now the Czech Republic.

Tony Esposito

43

Faceoff

Hockey is played between two teams of five skaters and a goalie. Each team has two defensemen and a forward line that includes a left wing, right wing, and center. The goalie's job is to stop the puck from crossing the red goal line. A hockey goal is 6 feet (1.8 meters) wide and 4 feet (1.2 meters) high. The hockey puck is a round disk made of hard rubber. It weighs approximately 6 ounces.

During a game, players work hard for a full "shift." When they get tired, they take a seat on the bench, and a new group jumps off the bench and over the boards to take their place (except for the goalie). Forwards play together in set groups, or "lines," and defensemen do, too.

There are rules that prevent players from injuring or interfering with opponents. However, players are allowed to bump, or "check," each other when they battle for the puck. Because hockey is a fast game played by strong athletes, sometimes checks can be rough!

If a player breaks a rule, a penalty is called by one of two referees. For most penalties, the player must sit in the penalty box for two minutes. This gives the other team a one-skater advantage, or "power play." The team down a skater is said to be "short-handed."

NHL games have three 20-minute periods—60 minutes in all—and the team that scores the most goals is the winner. If the score is tied, the teams play an overtime period. The first team to score during overtime wins. If the game is still tied, it is decided by a shootout—a one-on-one contest between the goalies and the best shooters from the other team. During the Stanley Cup playoffs, no shootouts are held. The teams play until the tie is broken.

Things happen so quickly in hockey that it is easy to overlook set plays. The next time you watch a game, see if you can spot these plays:

PLAY LIST

DEFLECTION—Sometimes a shooter does not try to score a goal. Instead, he aims his shot so that a teammate can touch the puck with his stick and suddenly change its direction. If the goalie is moving to stop the first shot, he may be unable to adjust to the "deflection."

GIVE-AND-GO—When a skater is closely guarded and cannot get an open shot, he sometimes passes to a teammate with the idea of getting a return pass in better position to shoot. The "give-and-go" works when the defender turns to follow the pass and loses track of his man. By the time he recovers, it is too late.

ONE-TIMER—When a player receives a pass, he often has to control the puck and position himself for a shot. This gives the defense a chance to react. Some players are skilled enough to shoot the instant a pass arrives for a "one-timer." A well-aimed one-timer is almost impossible to stop.

PULLING THE GOALIE—Sometimes in the final moments of a game, the team that is behind will try a risky play. To gain an extra skater, the team will pull the goalie out of the game and replace him with a center, wing, or defenseman. This gives the team a better chance to score. It also leaves the goal unprotected and allows the opponent a chance to score an "empty-net goal."

Glossary

HOCKEY WORDS TO KNOW

ALL-AROUND—Good at all parts of the game.

ALL-STAR—An award given to the league's best players at the end of each season.

ALL-STAR GAME—The annual game featuring the NHL's best players. Prior to 1967, the game was played at the beginning of the season between the league champion and an All-Star squad. Today it is played during the season. The game doesn't count in the standings.

ASSISTS—Passes that lead to a goal.

CHEMISTRY—The way players work together on and off the ice. Winning teams usually have good chemistry.

CLUTCH—Performing well under pressure.

DRAFT—The annual meeting during which NHL teams choose from a group of the best junior hockey, college, and international players. The draft is held each summer.

HALL OF FAME—The museum in Toronto, Canada where hockey's greatest players are honored. A player voted into the Hall of Fame is sometimes called a "Hall of Famer."

HAT TRICK—Three goals in one game.

HIPCHECKS—Checks that use a hip to knock an opponent off balance.

MINOR LEAGUER—A player who plays at a level below the NHL.

NATIONAL HOCKEY LEAGUE (NHL)—The league that began play in 1917–18 and is still in existence today.

OVERTIME—The extra period played when a game is tied after 60 minutes.

PLAYOFFS—The games played after the season to determine the league champion.

POSTSEASON—Another term for playoffs.

PROFESSIONAL—A player or team that plays a sport for money. College players are not paid, so they are considered "amateurs."

ROOKIE—A player in his first season.

SHUTOUTS—Games in which a team is prevented from scoring.

STANDINGS—A daily list of teams, starting with the team with the best record and ending with the team with the worst record.

STANLEY CUP—The championship trophy of North American hockey since 1893, and of the NHL since 1927.

STANLEY CUP FINALS—The series that determines the NHL champion each season. It has been a best-of-seven series since 1939.

VETERANS—Players with great experience.

VEZINA TROPHY—The award given to the league's top goalie each season.

WESTERN CONFERENCE FINALS—The series that determines which team from the West will face the best team from the East in the Stanley Cup Finals.

OTHER WORDS TO KNOW

AMPLIFY—Increase.

ANCHORED—Held steady.

ANVIL—A heavy iron block.

BURLY—Having a large, strong body.

CLICHÉ—A phrase used over and over again.

CONTENDER—A person or team that competes for a championship.

DECADES—Periods of 10 years; also specific periods, such as the 1950s.

ELECTRIFIED—Excited in a flashy way.

GENERATION—A group of people born during the same period of history.

INDESTRUCTIBLE—Impossible to wear down.

JUBILANT—Filled with great joy.

LOGO—A symbol or design that represents a company or team.

MASCOT—An animal or person believed to bring a group good luck.

SYNTHETIC—Made in a laboratory, not in nature.

TRADITION—A belief or custom that is handed down from generation to generation.

UNLEASHED—Let loose.

Places to Go

ON THE ROAD

CHICAGO BLACKHAWKS
1901 West Madison Street
Chicago, Illinois 60612
(312) 455-7000

THE HOCKEY HALL OF FAME
Brookfield Place
30 Yonge Street
Toronto, Ontario, Canada M5E 1X8
(416) 360-7765

ON THE WEB

THE NATIONAL HOCKEY LEAGUE www.nhl.com
- *Learn more about the National Hockey League*

THE CHICAGO BLACKHAWKS blackhawks.nhl.com
- *Learn more about the Blackhawks*

THE HOCKEY HALL OF FAME www.hhof.com
- *Learn more about hockey's greatest players*

ON THE BOOKSHELF

To learn more about the sport of football, look for these books at your library or bookstore:

- MacDonald, James. *Hockey Skills: How to Play Like a Pro*. Berkeley Heights, New Jersey: Enslow Elementary, 2009.
- Keltie, Thomas. *Inside Hockey! The legends, facts, and feats that made the game*. Toronto, Ontario, Canada: Maple Tree Press, 2008.
- Romanuk, Paul. *Scholastic Canada Book of Hockey Lists*. Markham, Ontario, Canada: Scholastic Canada, 2007.

Index

48

The Team

MARK STEWART has written over 200 books for kids—and more than a dozen books on hockey, including a history of the Stanley Cup and an authorized biography of goalie Martin Brodeur. He grew up in New York City during the 1960s rooting for the Rangers and now lives in New Jersey, where he attends Devils games at the new Prudential Center. He especially likes the special all-you-can-eat seating section. Mark comes from a family of writers. His grandfather was Sunday Editor of *The New York Times* and his mother was Articles Editor of *The Ladies' Home Journal* and *McCall's*. Mark has profiled hundreds of athletes over the last 20 years. He has also written several books about New York and New Jersey. Mark is a graduate of Duke University, with a degree in History. He lives with his daughters and wife Sarah overlooking Sandy Hook, New Jersey.

DENIS GIBBONS is a writer and editor with *The Hockey News* and a former newsletter editor of the Toronto-based Society for International Hockey Research (SIHR). He was a contributing writer to the publication *Kings of the Ice: A History of World Hockey* and has worked as chief hockey researcher at five Winter Olympics for the ABC, CBS, and NBC television networks. Denis also has worked as a researcher for the FOX Sports Network during the Stanley Cup playoffs. He resides in Burlington, Ontario, Canada with his wife Chris.